OCT 2 0 2008

Heart and Stomach
of a King

Heart and Stomach of a King

ENGLISH HERITAGE

First published in Great Britain in 2007 by
English Heritage • Kemble Drive • Swindon SN2 2GZ

Packaged by Susanna Geoghegan
Text copyright © Complete Editions

All rights reserved

ISBN 9781905624515

Printed in China by Hung Hing

Introduction

The future Queen Elizabeth I was born in September 1533 and learned from an early age that being a woman of royal blood in 16th-century England was perilous. For the first 25 years of her life, before she acceded to the throne, she walked a narrow line of personal security, threatened by the actions of those in authority over her, and was often the unwilling target of conspirators who saw her as the ideal figurehead for their particular cause. As a queen there was the ever-present risk of assassination, or execution following a successful coup against her. Yet, in spite of this, Elizabeth I established herself in the national conscience as 'Gloriana': the triumphant leader of her nation, who transformed a country bankrupt and in despair, into one which ranked among the most prosperous in Europe – and one that defied and vanquished the seemingly overwhelming might of Spain.

The Elizabethan age was an era of great men: Spenser, Marlowe and Shakespeare in the world of literature; Drake, Raleigh and Frobisher across the world as a whole; while at home, the wise counsel of Walsingham and Cecil guided and administered her government.

Elizabeth was the daughter of Henry VIII's second wife, Anne Boleyn. Henry's first wife Catherine of Aragon had only succeeded in providing Henry with a daughter, Mary. As Catherine grew older and the likelihood of her bearing a son diminished, Henry began to look elsewhere for a wife who could give him a male heir to ensure the survival of the Tudor royal line founded by his father, Henry VII.

Anne Boleyn appeared to be the answer. But in order to make her his wife, Henry had first to annul his marriage to Catherine, and the political and theological steps required to achieve this had far-reaching consequences. They led to England formally breaking away from the Catholic Church; to Henry replacing the pope as the supreme head of the Church of England; to the state acquisition and plunder of the more than 600 religious houses that had grown up in England over the centuries; and to religious strife that was to tear at the heart of the country for a century and a half.

It was little wonder that after all this Henry hoped his efforts would be rewarded with a son. But fate cheated him and three years after Elizabeth had been born her mother was executed to make way for Jane Seymour, the woman who did finally deliver the heir the king wanted.

As a child, Elizabeth knew and witnessed much sorrow, loneliness and bitterness. She was aware that sudden death was never far away: her mother's, that of two of her stepmothers (Jane Seymour, who died after giving birth to Elizabeth's half-brother Edward, and another stepmother, Catherine Howard, who was executed for adultery) and the deaths of a succession of 'traitors' sent to the scaffold to preserve Henry's reign. While much of her early life was spent as a virtual prisoner, it was profitably filled with inspired tutors, books and music – and by the company of her half-brother, four years her junior.

As Henry VIII's appointed heir, Edward VI became king of England when Henry died in 1547. His uncle, the duke of Somerset, had been appointed as protector, to administer the government of the country on behalf of the 10-year-old king. Next in the line of succession came Mary, and after her Elizabeth. However, across the English Channel, Mary Stuart, heiress to the throne of Scotland and granddaughter of Henry VIII's eldest sister, Margaret, had a stronger claim to the throne of England than either of the

Tudor princesses. Like Mary Tudor, though, Mary Stuart was a staunch Catholic and she also had a strong allegiance to France, both of which alienated the sympathies of most people in England.

All the same, after Henry's powerful presence, the next 11 years were characterised by plots, counter-plots, spying and political intrigue. Edward could exercise little power as king. His protector lacked his father's charisma and drive,and the nation suffered accordingly.

Fond as he was of Elizabeth and despite his father's efforts to guarantee the legality of her birth, Edward was persuaded that both Mary and she were illegitimate and therefore ineligible to sit on the throne. In their place he tried to ensure that the succession passed to Lady Jane Grey, the granddaughter of Henry VIII's younger sister Mary. Jane was two years younger than Elizabeth and, like her, highly educated – she was also a staunch Protestant. However, Edward's plan stood little chance of success and within a fortnight of his death Jane, her husband and her supporters were locked in the Tower and Mary Tudor was on the throne.

Mary and Elizabeth had little in common. Mary was old enough to be Elizabeth's mother and the differences in their respective faiths had driven

a wedge between them. Although Elizabeth conformed to Mary's edict that everyone at court should attend Mass, she quickly absented herself. Few believed that she had truly converted. For most people, Elizabeth remained the principal Protestant in the royal line and throughout her half-sister's reign she had to endure suspicion of involvement with secret Protestant resistance movements and periods of imprisonment.

By now Elizabeth, in her early twenties, was wary of displaying her feelings too openly. When she was 14 she had become involved in a flirtation with Thomas Seymour, younger brother of Edward VI's protector and the husband of Henry VIII's widow, Catherine Parr. This flirtation very nearly went too far and it took all of Elizabeth's intelligence and self-control to avoid nothing worse than intense interrogation; it cost Thomas Seymour his head, when he was found guilty of treachery for planning to marry the princess after his wife had died.

The death of Queen Mary in November 1558 came as a release for Elizabeth and for the country, torn by religious dissension and financially crippled. With no public office open to a woman except the Crown itself, Elizabeth had to juggle her duties as monarch with her status as a woman. In later life, as the Virgin Queen, she played this to advantage. But in the early years of her reign she found herself, predictably, prey to rumours and advances with a single objective in mind – her marriage.

From the start Queen Elizabeth I laid down a marker, leaving no one in doubt that her first loyalty was to the country and people she reigned over. She never felt the need of a husband's support in the business of ruling. She presided over a council of first-rate advisors and administrators she had chosen herself. She may have wished for emotional support, but the imperative driving her towards marriage was the same as her father's had been – the succession and the maintenance of their Tudor dynasty.

The topic of the queen's suitors provided endless speculation and gossip, but only three, or maybe four, of them were ever taken seriously. First was Robert Dudley, a friend Elizabeth had known from childhood but with whom she fell in love in 1559. Their close friendship sparked suggestions, almost certainly false, that he was her lover. Apart from not being her social equal, Dudley was a married man and it was far too risky for Elizabeth to take him to her bed. When Dudley's wife died in mysterious circumstances in 1560, Elizabeth was torn between personal desire and political expediency. Dudley was unpopular, particularly with Elizabeth's most trusted advisor, William Cecil (later Lord Burghley) and after months of anxious struggle her political instincts held sway. Dudley was created earl of Leicester and joined Elizabeth's privy council. For the rest of his life he retained a special place in the queen's affections but any chance of marriage to her had slipped away.

With the queen's passion curbed, the question of her marriage became one of foreign policy, in the course of which one foreign suitor stood out from the rest: Francis, Duke of Alençon and Anjou, the brother of the king of France. Between 1579 and 1581 the queen and the French prince pursued their affair against a background of diplomatic manoeuvring and negotiation. For all that, Elizabeth appeared genuinely interested in the personable and amusing young man.

Then duty intervened once again, as public opinion seemed set against the match, principally because the queen was thought to be beyond child-bearing age and would therefore be handing the country to a foreign power when she died, rather than to her successor. Elizabeth understood these concerns, reluctantly brought an end to the marriage discussions and began to be represented as the Virgin Queen from this point on; marriage, it appeared was no longer an option. Virginity was not simply a symbol of virtue and integrity, for Elizabeth it became a symbol of power.

The earl of Leicester died in 1588 and the gap he left in the queen's life was filled by his stepson, the earl of Essex. Thirty-three years younger than the queen, Essex was handsome and dashing, but unfortunately undisciplined and hugely ambitious. But the queen was amused by him and indulged his youthful excesses, much to the distaste of many at court. Lord Burghley, who had known the queen since she was a girl, suspected Essex's motives; he was proved right when his son, Robert Cecil, succeeded him as the queen's principal minister and Essex took this as a personal slight.

In 1599 Essex was sent to Ireland with a large force to put down the rebellion led by the earl of Tyrone and failed spectacularly, to the point where he deserted his command and returned to England without leave. The queen was livid and in retaliation Essex convinced himself and a small group of hangers-on that Robert Cecil was his nemesis and that the queen needed to be rescued from his pernicious influence. From there it was a short step to plotting to take control of the court and seize the queen herself. So deluded was he by this stage that Essex appeared to have little understanding of how fragile his support was. In February 1601 he made his move but the attempted uprising in London failed at the outset and by nightfall Essex and his supporters were arrested and in the Tower. He was executed within the month leaving the queen devastated, as much by the knowledge that her own conduct had led to his downfall as by having to authorise his execution.

Between her early infatuation for Robert Dudley and her willful indulgence of Essex, Elizabeth I oversaw the transformation of England. Through stringent economies and heavy taxation she restored the economy. She consolidated her father's work in establishing the Church of England and maintaining a well-equipped navy. She oversaw a burgeoning renaissance of literature, art, music and architecture. Under her patronage, English explorers ventured farther across the surface of the earth on land and sea than they had ever done before. And through skilful, though sometimes infuriatingly drawn-out, diplomacy she succeeded in establishing England as a significant world power, at a time when several of its adversaries were beginning to decline.

Set against these achievements of 'Gloriana', were the continuing political tensions and religious turmoil that lasted through most of her reign. The struggle between the newly established Protestant church and the deeply rooted Catholic traditions became personified in her cousin Mary, Queen of Scots. Elizabeth held no personal animosity towards her cousin but she could not risk any intimation that she recognised any claim to the throne made by a Catholic. So for 18 years Mary lived in England as Elizabeth's prisoner, after crossing the border from Scotland in 1568, seeking shelter after the defeat of her army at the battle of Langside near Glasgow.

During those 18 years a succession of plots to usurp the throne were hatched and uncovered. Elizabeth held out against removing Mary permanently from the political scene and even when, after one plot too many, she finally agreed to Mary's trial and execution, she gave the impression of having been forced, or even tricked, into sending her cousin to her death.

No doubt Elizabeth understood the consequences of executing a Catholic queen. For 25 years she had maintained peace with Catholic Spain, despite the repeated attacks on Spanish shipping by English adventurers. This understanding with Philip II had been achieved primarily by threatening him with Mary's claim to the throne coupled with her allegiance to France. If Philip attacked England, Elizabeth warned him, it would lead to an Anglo-French alliance against Spain, which was certainly not what Philip wanted.

But with Mary executed Elizabeth no longer held that card. A year later, Philip sent his invincible Armada to link up with Spanish forces in the Netherlands and invade England. The comprehensive defeat of the largest invasion force ever sent against her realm marked the high point of Elizabeth's reign. Always a powerful orator, the speech she gave to her troops, before victory was secured, stands alongside the greatest rallying cries and calls to arms ever delivered in the English language.

The nation she had given her life to build had been saved from destruction, but the queen herself went into gradual decline. Pride sustained her, even after the death of Essex, her wayward favourite. Almost exactly two years after he went to the block, Elizabeth herself died, on 24 March 1603.

There was no Tudor successor. The dynasty that had ruled England for over a century died with her. But her legacy has remained undimmed and when the young Queen Elizabeth II was crowned 350 years later, her reign was greeted as a new Elizabethan era as radiant and full of promise as that of her predecessor.

Affairs of State

'Do not tell secrets to those whose faith and silence you have not already tested.'

Elizabeth to Erik, king of Sweden, in 1561

⌒⤳

'Monarchs ought to put to death the authors and instigators of war, as their sworn enemies and as dangers to their states.'

Elizabeth to the French ambassador

⌒⤳

'There was never a woman born, for all respects, as Queen Elizabeth, for she spake and understood all languages; knew all estates and dispositions of princes. And particularly was so expert in the knowledge of her own realm and estate as no councillor she had could tell her what she knew not before.'

William Cecil, Lord Burghley

⌒⤳

'The past cannot be cured.'

Elizabeth to the Spanish ambassador

'If we still advise we shall never do.'

**Elizabeth to Sir Henry Sidney, on the question of what steps
to take in establishing English control of Ireland**

Assassination Attempts

The risk of attack was ever present. On one occasion the queen was being rowed on the River Thames when a man in a nearby boat fired a gun at her, missing the queen, but wounding one of the royal oarsmen. Giving no thought to her own safety, she pulled off the scarf she was wearing and used it to bind the man's bleeding arm, telling him not to be afraid because she would take care of him.

'The many evil plots and designs have overcome all her Highness' sweet temper. She walks much in her privy Chamber, and stamps with her feet at ill news, and thrusts her rusty sword at times into the arras in great rage … The dangers are over, and yet she always keeps a sword by her table.'

Sir John Harington, Queen Elizabeth's godson

Beauty Treatments

Elizabeth I was tall and striking, with pale skin and light red-gold hair. As such she conformed to the Renaissance ideal of feminine beauty, which favoured fair hair, bright eyes, red lips and a pale complexion – the hallmark of a noble lady, who did not have to labour outside like her tanned and weather-beaten sisters.

Achieving an alabaster complexion called for many substances that could have a serious long-term impact on the user's health. The most widely used skin foundation was a paste called ceruse, which was made from white lead and vinegar. In addition sulphur, mercury and turpentine were key ingredients in concoctions applied to the skin to bleach freckles and treat blemishes. Regular use of these cosmetics had a disastrous effect on the very complexions they were intended to enhance – 'grey and shrivelled' was the verdict of one contemporary commentator. However, other treatments were at hand to remedy this, including raw egg white, which was painted onto the face to produce a smooth, marble-like complexion.

When it came to the queen's hair, there were other fearsome treatments for dyeing and bleaching, with red wigs a popular alternative.

Such was the queen's influence on the style and fashion of her day that when her legendary sweet tooth caused her teeth to decay, many women slavishly followed her appearance and blackened their otherwise healthy teeth to look like her.

Be My Guest

Winning favour in the eyes of Queen Elizabeth frequently involved entertaining Her Majesty and her extensive retinue on her royal progresses through the country at enormous expense. It is said that when Lord Burghley entertained the queen and her companions on one occasion, that three-day visit alone cost him between £2,000 and £3,000.

In some instances the expense involved went as far as building a brand new house. Sir William More, a favourite advisor to Elizabeth I, was told by the queen that she wished to stay at his home, except that the old medieval house in which he lived with his family 'was not mete for her to tarry at'.

Sir William More was not a wealthy man – however he took the hint and set about building a new home better suited to royal entertainment. Four years and £1,640 19s 7d later it was ready. The queen showed her approval by visiting on four occasions; even so, she could be a demanding guest. In one letter to Sir William she gave instructions for the drive to be strewn with straw to reduce the jolting of her carriage. She also made the pointed comment that the house should be cleaner than it had been when she last visited.

Not content with making these demands, when the royal party arrived Sir William and his household were required to move out of their new home to take up temporary residence in the old medieval house, which had wisely been retained to provide over-flow accommodation.

Benefits in Kind

As Queen Elizabeth's favourite, Sir Walter Raleigh lost no opportunity to gather benefits and rewards.

His rapacity was not lost on the queen, who once rebuked him mildly, asking, 'When will you cease to be a beggar?'

'When you cease to be a benefactress, ma'am,' Raleigh told her.

A Breach of Decorum

On one occasion, Edward de Vere, the earl of Oxford, suffered the acute embarrassment of audibly breaking wind when he bowed low to Queen Elizabeth. He was so ashamed of his behaviour that he left England and travelled abroad for several years. On his return home he went to court to pay his respects to the queen, who welcomed him back and said, 'My lord, I had forgotten the fart.'

Command Performance

The theatrical tradition that Elizabeth I personally commissioned Shakespeare to write *The Merry Wives of Windsor* was first mentioned by the critic and playwright John Dennis, in the preface to his adaptation of the play, which was published in 1702.

'That this Comedy was not despicable, I guess'd for several Reasons: First, I knew very well, that it had pleas'd one of the greatest Queens that ever was in the World … This Comedy was written at her Command, and by her direction, and she was so eager to see it Acted, that she commanded it to be finished in fourteen days and was afterwards, as Tradition tells us, very well pleas'd at the Representation.'

Dangerous Dalliances

One of the lessons that Elizabeth learned as a teenager was the importance of public perception of her character and conduct. After the death of her father, she and her older half-sister, Mary, were living in the household of their stepmother, Catherine Parr. By this time Catherine had been married three times and always to elderly or impotent husbands. So, when a former suitor only a year or two older than herself began to renew his attention, she responded warmly.

The man in question was Thomas Seymour, the younger brother of the duke of Somerset, who had been appointed lord protector by Henry VIII, to govern the country when his young son Edward VI acceded to the throne. It is thought that he and Catherine Parr had been planning to marry after the death of her second husband, but the king had stepped in and married her himself. Now Henry was dead Seymour pursued his advances, even though he knew they would displease his brother.

However, he had developed a reputation as a ladies' man and is reported to have made passes at both the princesses before settling on their stepmother. Mary, who was 31 by now, left immediately and set up an establishment of her own leaving Elizabeth, half her age, with Catherine and her new husband. The 14-year-old girl appears to have been very taken with Thomas Seymour who began going into Elizabeth's chamber some mornings wearing just his nightshirt. Worse still, there were occasions when he climbed into bed with her and tickled her.

Perhaps fortunately for Elizabeth, these frolics were prevented from going further when Seymour was caught by his wife embracing Elizabeth in compromising circumstances. The young princess was packed off to one of her own houses right away, leaving Sir Thomas to patch things up with his wife.

In spite of her timely departure, Elizabeth's behaviour, innocent or not, had made her vulnerable to rumour and gossip. After Catherine Parr died in childbirth, Seymour began to pursue Elizabeth again, this time with suggestions of marriage. As Elizabeth was the king's half-sister and second in the line of succession (after Mary), this would never have been permitted. Even so, when Thomas Seymour was arrested on suspicion of planning a coup against his brother, one of the charges against him was that he was plotting to marry the king's sister. From this spread rumours that he had seduced Princess Elizabeth, that she was pregnant by him and that she herself had been arrested.

None of this was true, of course, and Elizabeth behaved with great maturity for a 15-year-old when she was rigorously interrogated about the affair. But it was an early lesson in the impact her marriage prospects, not to mention her emotions, would have on her life as an adult and a queen.

Defeating the Spanish Armada

The execution of Mary, Queen of Scots in February 1587 gave Philip II of Spain the excuse he was looking for to invade Protestant England. The 'invincible' armada that he assembled sailed from Lisbon in May 1588 under the command of the duke of Medina Sidonia. His orders were to win control of the English Channel and then convey the duke of Parma's invasion force of 30,000 men from the Netherlands across the Channel. In the event, his huge naval force became trapped in Calais Roads in August 1588 and was dispersed in confusion by English fireships. A naval battle fought off Gravelines produced an English victory thanks to superior long-range gunfire, after which the long-awaited threat of invasion disappeared in autumn gales. An account of the action written by Sir William Winter gives an eyewitness account of what happened at the key moments of the battle.

'The Spanish Army [the armada] was anchored to the eastward of Calais cliffs, very round and near together not far from the shore, our army not being past a mile and a half behind them … having viewed the great and hugeness of the Spanish Army and did consider that it was not possible to move them but by the device of firing of ships, which would make them lose the only rode [anchorage] which was apt and meet for their purpose … Upon Sunday being the 28th day my Lord [the English admiral, Howard of Effingham] put out his flag of council early, the Armies both riding still, and after the assembly of the council it was concluded that the practice for the firing of ships should be put in execution the night following … So at about twelve of the clock that night six ships were brought and prepared … having the wind and tide with them and their ordnance being charged were fired, and the men that were the executors, so soon as the fire was made they abandoned the ships and entered into five boats that were appointed for the saving of them. This matter did put such terror amongst the Spanish Army that they were fain [obliged] to let slip their cables and anchors and did work as it did appear great mischief amongst them … about ix of the clock in the morning we fell into position, then being within the water of Gravelines. They went into the proportion of the half moon, their admiral and vice-admiral were in the midst and their greatest vessels and power were one upon the other … The fight continued from ix of the clock until 6 of the clock at night, in which time the Spanish Army bear away NNE and N by E as many as they could keeping company with one another … Great was the spoil and harm that was done to them no doubt.'

Distant Cousins

An interesting irony surrounding the two most charismatic women living in the British Isles during the second half of the 16th century is that Elizabeth, queen of England, and her cousin, Mary, Queen of Scots never met. Elizabeth 'attended' the christening of Mary's son, who would succeed her as King James I of England, by proxy: a royal representative was dispatched with a baptismal font. On numerous occasions while she held her prisoner Elizabeth promised to visit Mary, but no visit ever materialised. Even at Mary's funeral the countess of Bedford stood in for the queen of England.

However, the two queens were perversely united after death. Today, both of them lie buried in the Lady Chapel of Westminster Abbey: Elizabeth on the north side of the nave, Mary on the south side.

Dudley's Farewell

Robert Dudley, earl of Leicester, wrote this letter to Elizabeth I on 29 August 1588 and she kept it among her possessions for the final 15 years of her life, endorsed with the note 'his last letter', for Dudley was to die a few days later on 4 September.

'I most humbly beseech your Majesty to pardon your poor old servant to be thus bold in sending to know how my gracious lady does, and what ease of her late pain she finds, being the chiefest thing in the world that I do pray for, for her to have good health and long life. For my own poor case I continue still your medicine and find it amends much better than any other thing that hath been given me. Thus hoping to find perfect cure at the bath, with the continuance of my wonted [usual] prayer for your Majesty's most happy preservation, I humbly kiss your foot. From your old lodging at Rycote this Thursday morning, ready to take my journey,

by your Majesty's most faithful and obedient servant
R. Leicester'

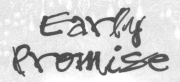

Early Promise

'If she be no more educated than she now appeareth to me, she will prove of no less honour and womanhood, than shall beseem her father's daughter.'

Sir Thomas Wriothesley on meeting the 6-year-old Elizabeth in 1539

Elizabethan Legacy

'She brought England through a very perilous passage into smooth waters. Unfortunately for her successors the chart by which she steered her erratic course was destroyed with her death.'

Conyers Read, *The Tudors*

Eternal Youth

Very few artists had the opportunity to paint the queen from life – most worked from approved 'face patterns' derived from official portraits. As she aged, her image was more tightly controlled, with an official proclamation of 1596 ordering any 'unseemly' portraits to be destroyed. This served a double purpose. Presenting the queen as eternally youthful was flattering as far as she was concerned. The appearance of eternal youth carried with it the suggestion of long life, which suggested stability and constancy, and neatly sidestepped questions of what might happen to the country when the queen died.

The Etiquette of Gaining an Audience

Catching the queen when she was in a good mood was the only way of successfully placing a petition before her. 'When her Highness is angry or not well disposed, trouble not with any matter which you desire to have done,' ran the advice given as guidance to anyone with matters they wished to raise with the queen.

However, there were some at court who had developed their own ways of approaching her. One was her godson, Sir John Harington, who followed this course of action:

'I must go in an early hour, before her highness hath special matters brought to counsel on. I must go before the breakfasting covers are placed, and stand uncovered as her Highness cometh forth her chamber; then kneel, and say, "God save your Majesty! I crave your ear at what hour may suit for your servant to meet your blessed countenance?" Thus will I gain her favour to the auditory.'

Favourite of the Queen

For ten years Sir Walter Raleigh was the queen's great favourite and she was said 'to love this gentleman now beyond all others'. However, that love can best be described as no more than a fascination with the witty, adventurous courtier on Elizabeth's part, despite ardent sentiments, like these, that he expressed for her:

> *O eyes that pierce our hearts without remorse,*
> *O hairs of right that wear a royal crown,*
> *O hands that conquer more than Caesar's force*

O wit that turns huge kingdoms upside down!
Then Love, be judge, what heart may thee withstand!
Such eyes, such hair, such wit, and such a hand!

Global Expansion

During the reign of Elizabeth I, British trade underwent a worldwide expansion, thanks in large measure to enterprising merchants seeking new markets, a new school of skilful mariners, and adventurous explorers by land as well as sea. In 1589 the English geographer and historian, Richard Hakluyt, proudly acknowledged their achievements in the opening to the first edition of his three-volume work *Principal Navigations, Voyages, and Discoveries of the English Nation.*

'Which of the Kings of this land before her Majesty, had their banners ever seen in the Caspian sea? Which of them hath ever dealt with the Emperor of Persia as her Majesty hath done, and obtained for her merchants large and loving privileges? Who ever saw, before this regiment, an English Ligier in the stately porch of the Grand Signor at Constantinople? Who ever found English Consuls and Agents at Tripoli in Syria, at Aleppo, at Babylon, at Bakara, and, which is more, who ever heard of Englishmen at Goa before now? What English ship had heretofore ever anchor in the mighty river of Plate? Pass and repass the unpassable (in former opinion) strait of Magellan, range along the coast of Chili, Peru and all the backside of Nova Hispania, further than any Christian ever passed, traverse the mighty breadth of the South Sea, land upon the Luzones, in despite of the enemy, enter into alliance, amity and traffic with the Princes of Maluccas, and the isle of Java, double the famous Cape of Bona Speranza, arrive at the isle of St Helena, and last of all return home richly laden with the commodities of China, as the subjects of this now flourishing monarch have done?'

Gloriana at 64

On 8 December 1597, André Hurault, the French ambassador to England, was granted a private audience with Elizabeth I. The account he kept of that meeting provides a fascinating description of the queen at the age of 64, a little over five years before her death.

'I drew near to her chair and began to deal with her in that wherewithal I had been charged; and because I was uncovered, from time to time she signed to me with her hand to be covered, which I did. Soon after she caused a stool to be brought, whereon I sat and began to talk to her.

She was strangely attired in a dress of silver cloth, white and crimson, of silver "gauze", as they call it. This dress had slashed sleeves lined with red taffeta, and was girt about with other little sleeves that hung down to the ground, which she was for ever twisting … The collar of the robe was very high, and the lining of the inner part all adorned with little pendants of rubies and pearls, very many, but quite small. She had also a chain of rubies and pearls about her neck. On her head she wore a garland of rubies and pearls, and beneath it a great reddish-coloured wig, with a great number of pearls, not of great worth. On either side of her ears hung two great curls of hair, almost down to her shoulders and within the collar of her robe, spangled like the top of her head. Her bosom was rather wrinkled … As for her face it is … long and thin, and her teeth are very yellow and irregular … on the left side less than the right. Many of them are missing, so that you cannot understand her easily when she speaks quickly. Her figure is fair and tall and graceful in whatever she does; so far as may be she keeps her dignity, yet humbly and graciously withal.'

Going up in Smoke

'I have known many persons who turned their gold into smoke, but you are the first to turn smoke into gold.'

Elizabeth to Sir Walter Raleigh, on his introduction of tobacco into England

Good and Faithful Servant

'This judgement I have of you, that you will not be corrupted by any manner of gifts, and that you will be faithful to the State; and that without respect of any private will, you will give me the counsel you think best.'

Elizabeth to William Cecil on making him secretary of state at her accession

'Must! Is must a word to be addressed to princes? Little man, little man! thy father, if he had been alive, durst not have used that word.'

Spoken by Elizabeth to Robert Cecil (son of William) towards the end of her life

Good Queen Bess

'She was received everywhere with great acclamation and signs of joy, as is customary in this country, whereat she was exceedingly pleased and told me so, giving me to understand how beloved she was by her subjects and how highly she esteemed this … She would order her carriage some-times to be taken where the crowd seemed thickest and stood up and thanked her people.'

The Spanish ambassador, on Queen Elizabeth's popularity on a visit to Berkshire

Greeting Gloriana

In the middle of July 1575, Elizabeth I was sumptuously entertained at Kenilworth Castle in Warwickshire, in a manner which she had no doubt come to expect from wealthy noblemen who were seeking her favour and their own personal advancement. As an eyewitness, Robert Laneham, carefully noted down, the welcoming festivities began well before the royal party entered the castle.

'It was eight o'clock in the evening e'er her Highness came to Kenilworth; where, in the Park, about a flight-shot from the Brase and first gate of the Castle, one of the Sybils comely clad in a pall of white silk pronounced a proper poesie in English rhyme and meter …

This, her Majesty benignly accepting, passed forth unto the next gate of the Brase … where the Lady of the Lake, with two Nymphs waiting upon her, arrayed all in silks attended her Highness's coming, from the midst of the Pool, where, upon a movable island, bright blazing with torches, she, floating to land, met her Majesty with a well-penned meter … This pageant was closed up with a delectable harmony of Hautbois, Shalms, Cornets, and such other loud music, that held on till her Majesty pleasantly so passed from thence toward the Castle gate, whereunto … was framed a fair Bridge … railed on either part with posts … Upon the first pair of posts were set two comely square wire cages … In them live Bitterns, Curlews, Shovellers, Herons … and suchlike dainty Birds, of the presents of Sylvanus, the God of Fowls.

On the second pair, two great silvered bowls … filled with Apples, Pears, Cherries, Filberts, Walnuts, fresh upon their branches, and with Oranges, Pomegranates, Lemons, and Pippins, all for the gifts of Pomona, Goddess of Fruits. The third pair of posts, in two such silvered bowls, had (all in ears, green and gold), Wheat, Barley, Oats, Beans, and Peas, as the gifts of Ceres.

The fourth on the left hand, in a like silvered bowl, had Grapes in Clusters, white and red, graced by their Vine leaves. The corresponding post had a pair of great, white silver livery pots, for wine, and before them two glasses of good capacity … and these for the potential presents of Bacchus, the God of Wine.

The fifth pair had each a large tray strewed a little with fresh grass, and in them Conger, Burt, Mullet, fresh Herring, Oysters, Salmon, Crayfish, and such like, from Neptune, God of the Sea.'

Guarding the Queen's Person

Throughout her reign Elizabeth I lived in fear of assassination from the agents of foreign powers as well as from home-grown fanatics. As a result, she was seldom allowed to be alone. At night, one of her ladies slept in her chamber with her and four chambermaids were kept on permanent call, day and night. During the day, 50 or more gentlemen pensioners were stationed on duty to guard her.

Half-sister to the Queen

The relationship between the half-sisters, Mary and Elizabeth, had always been tense. Since her youth, Mary had harboured a deep enmity for Elizabeth's mother, Anne Boleyn, whom she blamed for her own mother's tragic fate and the alienation of her father's affection. Then there was religion: Mary was a devout Catholic, like her mother; Elizabeth was a Protestant, like hers.

When Mary acceded, however, she was prepared to be conciliatory. When she rode to her coronation, Elizabeth followed, accompanied by their father's fourth discarded wife, Anne of Cleves. Seen together, Henry VIII's two daughters were strikingly different. Elizabeth at 19 was tall and dressed in the severe clothes she adopted in her youth. Mary by contrast, was shorter, looked older than her 37 years and was richly adorned in velvet, jewels and gold.

Despite her outer display of sisterly affection, Mary remained deeply suspicious of Elizabeth and what she represented. For her, it was simply impossible to forget the past. Elizabeth responded by retreating from court and keeping her distance from the political intrigues that coloured Mary's reign.

The Venetian ambassador was a shrewd observer who recorded the following description of Mary I.

'She is of low rather than of middling stature, but, although short, she has not personal defect in her limbs, nor is any part of her body deformed. She is of spare and delicate frame, quite unlike her father, who was tall and stout; nor does she resemble her mother, who, if not tall, was nevertheless bulky. Her face is well formed, as shown by her features and lineaments, and as seen by her portraits. When younger she was considered, not merely tolerably handsome, but of beauty exceeding mediocrity. At present, with the exception of some wrinkles, caused more by anxieties than by age, which makes her appear some years older, her aspect, for the rest, is very grave. Her eyes are so piercing that they inspire not only respect, but fear in those on whom she fixes them, although she is very short-sighted, being unable to read or do anything else unless she has her sight quite close to what she wishes to peruse or to see distinctly. Her voice is rough and loud, almost like a man's, so that when she speaks she is always heard a long way off. In short, she is a seemly woman, and never to be loathed for ugliness, even at her present age, without considering her degree of queen. But whatever may be the amount deducted from her physical endowments, as much more may with truth, and without flattery, be added to those of her mind, as, besides the facility and quickness of her understanding, which comprehends whatever is intelligible to others, even to those who are not of her own sex (a marvellous gift for a woman), she is skilled in five languages, not merely understanding, but speaking four of them fluently – English, Latin, French, Spanish, and Italian, in which last, however, she does not venture to converse, although it is well known to her; but the replies she gives in Latin, and her very intelligent remarks made in that tongue, surprise everybody … '

Her Father's Daughter

'Proud and haughty, as although she knows she was born of such a mother, she nevertheless does not consider herself of inferior degree to the Queen [Mary], whom she equals in self-esteem; nor does she believe herself less legitimate than her Majesty, alleging in her own favour that her mother would never cohabit with the King unless by way of marriage, with the authority of the Church …

She prides herself on her father and glories in him; everybody saying that she also resembles him more than the Queen does and he therefore always liked her and had her brought up in the same way as the Queen.'

**Giovanni Michiel, the Venetian ambassador, describing
Princess Elizabeth in the spring of 1557**

Her Majesty's Hose

In 1561 Queen Elizabeth was presented with a pair of silk knit stockings by her silk-woman, Mrs Montague, and thenceforth she never wore cloth hose any more.

William Howell, *An Institution of General History*

The silk knit stockings were one of a long list of gifts traditionally given to the queen at the New Year by everyone from her highest ministers to the humblest employee. The presents were recorded on a great roll. Few of the rolls have survived, but one for 1596–7 was auctioned in London in 1967 and contained such items as a cloak of 'black Velvett the grounde gold with a flatte lace of Venis silver' from Lord Bacon, and some plums, a box of lozenges and 'a confusion of marzipan' from less illustrious subjects. So many gifts were recorded that the roll extended to 13 feet in length.

Her Majesty's Toilet

Elizabeth I was remarkable among people of her day, the nobility as well as the rest of her subjects, for her attention to personal hygiene. The rest of the court regarded her as being uncommonly fastidious and looked with quiet amazement at her habit of taking a bath once a month 'whether she needed it or no'. However, the queen's godson, the poet Sir John Harington, was regarded as being even more eccentric in taking a bath every day. For most Elizabethans, dirt and its attendant odours were part of life. This was particularly true of the primitive arrangements they had to endure when making calls of nature.

However, Harington set about improving this as far as his own house was concerned and in 1589 installed at his county seat, Kelston, near Bath, the first water-closet as we would recognise it in England. This was built according to Harington's own design and so pleased was he with the result that seven years later he published a description, diagram and list of items needed to construct his new invention for a total cost of 30 shillings and six pence. His godmother was evidently hugely impressed with the innovation and commissioned one for her own use at Richmond Palace. Sadly for Harington, though, this invention was a good couple of centuries ahead of its time and no one else took up the idea, even though it provided all the convenience of a modern flush lavatory including an airlock to obstruct foul odours rising from the waste pipe.

He Who Pays the Piper

Colly Cibber, the 18th-century actor, playwright and (from 1730) poet laureate, recorded this anecdote of the Elizabethan poet, Edmund Spenser.

'It is said that upon his presenting some poems to the Queen she ordered him a gratuity of one hundred pounds, but the Lord Treasurer Burleigh objecting to it, said with some scorn of the poet, of whose merit he was totally ignorant, "What, all this for a song?" The Queen replied, "Then give him what is reason." Spenser for some time waited, but had the mortification to find himself disappointed of Her Majesty's bounty. Upon this he took a proper opportunity to present a paper to Queen Elizabeth, in which he reminded her of the order she had given, in the following lines:

I was promised on a time
To have reason for my rhime.
From that time, unto this season,
I received nor rhime, nor reason.

The paper produced the intended effect, and the Queen, after sharply reproving the Treasurer, immediately directed the payment of the hundred pounds she had first ordered.'

Home Sweet Home

Queen Elizabeth I became accustomed to the nobles at court vying with each other to offer lavish entertainment when Her Majesty came to stay. So she was more than a little surprised to find that the keeper of the great seal, Nicholas Bacon, lived comparatively moderately at his house at Gorhambury in Hertfordshire.

'What a little house you have gotten,' remarked the queen somewhat disdainfully.

'The house is well,' replied Bacon, adding with consummate tact, 'but it is you, Your Majesty, who have made me too great for my house.'

Home Thoughts From Abroad

After the failure of the Catholic-inspired rebellion in the North, Catholics became associated with treachery and suffered accordingly. New laws disbarred them from becoming members of Parliament and also deprived Catholics of the opportunity to take up any form of government service or to become university teachers. As a result, many chose voluntary exile abroad to persecution at home. But this could be a lonely existence as an inscription in the church of San Gregorio in Rome testifies:

'Here lies Robert Peckham, Englishman and Catholic, who, after England's break with the Church, left England because he would not live in his country without the Faith, and, having come to Rome, died there because he could not live apart from his country.'

Imprisonment

'That milkmaid's lot is better than mine, and her life merrier.'
Elizabeth to one of her attendants, while imprisoned by her sister, Queen Mary, in 1554

In God We Trust

'Twas God the word that spake it,
He took the bread and brake it;
And what the word did make it;
That I believe, and take it.

Reputedly spoken by Elizabeth when questioned on her beliefs on the Eucharist in Mary's reign

'There is one thing higher than Royalty: and that is religion, which causes us to leave the world, and seek God.'

Elizabeth to her ladies-in-waiting.

'From the very beginning of her reign she has treated all religious questions with so much caution and incredible prudence that she seems both to protect the Catholic religion and at the same time not entirely to condemn or outwardly reject the new Reformation ... In my opinion, a very prudent action, intended to keep the adherents of both creeds in subjection, for the less she ruffles them at the beginning of her reign the more easily she will enthrall them later on.'

The imperial envoy Count von Helffstein, March 1559

'There is only one Christ, Jesus, one faith. All else is a dispute over trifles.'
Elizabeth responding to the Catholic/Protestant divide

'He that will forget God, will also forget his benefactors.'
Elizabeth to William Lambarde, 1601

Intellectual Pursuits

As a princess Elizabeth enjoyed advantages denied to all but a small number of Tudor children of her age. However, she was even more fortunate, as a girl, to receive a first-class education – and for this she had her stepmother Catherine Parr to thank. Elizabeth's father, Henry VIII, had entrusted Catherine, his sixth and last wife, to take care of the education of his two youngest children: Elizabeth and her half-brother Edward. Catherine Parr was an educated woman herself and she encouraged her lively and intelligent stepdaughter to develop her intellectual potential to the full, as well as acquiring skills, such as dancing and needlework, which were expected of a woman of royal standing.

In the 16th century it was customary to give presents at New Year rather than at Christmas and at the end of December 1545, when she was 12, Elizabeth sent her stepmother a translation she had made from French into English of the *Institutes* written by John Calvin, the French theologian and religious reformer; this was accompanied by a letter in French. At the same time her father received from her a translation which Elizabeth had made into Latin of his wife's own 'Prayer and meditations', which was also accompanied by a letter she had written to him in Latin.

As well as being fluent in Latin and French, the 12-year-old princess also spoke Italian and was making impressive progress with Greek.

The Irish Question

In the spring of 1599 the earl of Essex was sent to Ireland with a large army to bring to justice the rebellious earl of Tyrone, who had been plotting with Irish rebels and Spanish agents against Elizabeth I. As this letter from the queen states, Essex had squandered time and resources and incurred her displeasure as a result:

'We have perceived by your letters to our Council brought by Henry Carey that you are arrived at Dublin after your journey into Munster, where though it seems by the words of your letter that you have spent divers days in taking account of all things that have passed since you left that place yet have you in this dispatch given us small light either when or in what order you intend particularly to proceed to the northern action. Wherein if you compare the time that is run on and in the excessive charges that is spent with the effects of anything wrought by this voyage (howsoever we may remain satisfied with your own particular cares and travails of body and mind), yet you must needs think that we have the eyes of foreign princes upon our actions and have the hearts of people to comfort and cherish – who groan under the burden of continual levies and impositions which are occasioned by these late actions – can little please ourself hitherto with anything that has been effected …'

Jewels Fit For a Queen

As Elizabeth's love of clothes and jewellery became common knowledge, they became increasingly common New Year's gifts. On 1 January 1587, for example, Elizabeth received over 80 pieces of jewellery and she also received magnificent jewellery from her many suitors. From the inventory compiled by Mrs Blanche Parry, on her retirement in 1587 as Elizabeth's lady of the bedchamber, we know that Elizabeth had 628 pieces of jewellery at that time.

Just Deserts

'…It is true that the world was made in six days, but it was by God, to whose power the infirmity of men is not to be compared.'

Elizabeth replying to the French ambassador when he complained about waiting six days for an answer concerning her possible marriage to a French prince

A King of England Too

When the Spanish Armada threatened to invade England in the summer of 1588, an army was assembled at Tilbury in the Thames estuary to repel the force that was anticipated to land from across the English Channel. Elizabeth I travelled there to visit her troops and delivered this famous speech, to give them heart in the defence of her realm and their homeland.

'My loving people,

We have been persuaded by some that are careful of our safety, to take heed how we commit our selves to armed multitudes, for fear of treachery; but I assure you I do not desire to live to distrust my faithful and loving people. Let tyrants fear, I have always so behaved myself that, under God, I have placed my chiefest strength and safeguard in the loyal hearts and good-will of my subjects; and therefore I am come amongst you, as you see, at this time, not for my recreation and disport, but being resolved, in the midst and heat of the battle, to live and die amongst you all; to lay down for my God, and for my kingdom, and my people, my honour and my blood, even in the dust. I know I have the body but of a weak and feeble woman; but I have the heart and stomach of a king, and of a king of England too, and think foul scorn that Parma or Spain, or any prince of Europe, should dare to invade the borders of my realm; to which rather than any dishonour shall grow by me, I myself will take up arms, I myself will be your general, judge, and rewarder of every one of your virtues in the field. I know already, for your forwardness you have deserved rewards and crowns; and We do assure you in the word of a prince, they shall be duly paid you. In the mean time, my lieutenant general shall be in my stead, than whom never prince commanded a more noble or worthy subject; not doubting but by your obedience to my general, by your concord in the camp, and your valour in the field, we shall shortly have a famous victory over those enemies of my God, of my kingdom, and of my people.'

On Kingship

'What a family is without a steward, a ship without a pilot, a flock without a shepherd, a body without a head, the same, I think, is a kingdom without the health and safety of a good monarch.'

Elizabeth to her brother, King Edward, around 1550

Know Thyself

'They are most deceived that trusteth most in themselves.'

Elizabeth to Edward Seymour, lord protector of King Edward, 1549

'No crooked leg, no bleared eye,
No part deformed out of kind,
Nor yet so ugly half can be
As is the inward suspicious mind.'

Written by Elizabeth in her French book of Psalms

'There is no marvel in a woman learning to speak, but there would be in teaching her to hold her tongue.'

Elizabeth to the French ambassador after he had praised her linguistic skills

'I will have here but one mistress and no master.'

Elizabeth to Robert Dudley

'A clear and innocent conscience fears nothing.'

Elizabeth to the Spanish ambassador

'There is small disproportion betwixt a fool who useth not wit because he hath it not and him that useth it not when it should avail him.'

To Baron Buckhurst (Thomas Sackville, 1st earl of Dorset), around 1587

The Ladder of Success

Early in his career as a courtier, Sir Walter Raleigh used a diamond to scratch these words on a window in the royal palace, where he knew Queen Elizabeth would read them: 'Fain would I climb, yet I fear to fall'. As he had hoped, the Queen did spot them, although her reaction may not have been what he intended. For the queen completed the couplet with a diamond inscription of her own, 'If thy heart fail thee, climb not at all'.

Love of the Chase

Elizabeth I enjoyed hunting and falconry throughout her life and as late as 1600, when she was 67, it was recorded that, 'Her Majesty is well disposed to hunting, for every second day she is on horse-back and continues sport long.'

Maintaining Standards

Dress was a means of expressing social hierarchy in Elizabethan England and the queen firmly believed that one's dress should suit, but not exceed, one's rank. Elizabeth's appearance stressed her rank as head of state and church and 'pecking order' was reinforced by legal restrictions known as 'sumptuary laws', which set down strict guidelines, such as these issued at Greenwich on 15 June, 1574: 'None shall wear: Any cloth of gold, tissue, nor fur of sables: except duchesses, marquises, and countesses in their gowns, kirtles, partlets, and sleeves; cloth of gold, silver, tinseled satin, silk, or cloth mixed or embroidered with gold or silver or pearl, saving silk mixed with gold or silver in linings of cowls, partlets, and sleeves: except all degrees above viscountesses, and baronesses, and other personages of like degrees in their kirtles and sleeves …'

Married to her Realm

Parliamentary pressure for Elizabeth I to marry ensued in early 1559, when the House of Commons entered its plea for her to choose a husband. The historian William Camden recorded Parliament's request:

'There is nothing which with more ardent affection we beg of God in our daily prayers, than our happiness hitherto received by your most gratious government may be perpetuated to the English nation unto all eternity. Whilst in our mind and cogitation we cast many ways how this might be effected, we can find none at all, unless your Majesty shall reign for ever, or else by Marriage bring forth children, Heirs both to their Mother's Vertue and Empire. This is the single, the onely, the all-comprehending prayer of all Englishmen.'

In answer to this Elizabeth delivered her famous reply:

'… now that the Publick Care of governing the Kingdom is laid upon me, to draw upon me also the Cares of marriage may seem a point of inconsiderate Folly. Yea, to satisfie you, I have already joyned myself in marriage to an Husband, namely, the Kingdom of England … And to me it shall be a Full satisfaction, both for the memorial of my Name, and for my Glory also, if when I shall let my last breath, it be ingraven upon my Marble Tomb, "Here lieth Elizabeth, which Reigned a Virgin, and died a Virgin".'

Mary's Maladies

In spite of her widely acclaimed beauty, Mary, Queen of Scots seems to have been prey to a remarkable number of medical complaints and illnesses. The catalogue compiled by her biographers note that she suffered from: nervous collapses, hysteria, depression, smallpox, measles, influenza, liver disease, vomiting, indigestion, fevers, convulsions, rheumatism, chlorosis, consumption, gastric ulcers, porphyria and, towards the end of her life, permanent lameness.

Mistress of the Art – Elizabeth I's Love of Dancing

'She takes great pleasure in dancing and music. In her youth she danced very well and composed measures and music and had played them herself and danced them. She takes such pleasure in it that when her maids dance she follows the cadence with her hand and foot. She rebukes them if they do not dance to her liking and without a doubt she is mistress of the art, having learnt in the Italian manner to dance high.'

Note on Elizabeth I's love of dancing by a French diplomat in 1598

Monopolies Commissioned

During her reign Elizabeth I granted monopolies to certain individuals, which gave them the exclusive right to manufacture or trade in particular commodities. So the celebrated composers of her reign, William Byrd and Thomas Tallis, were granted a 21-year monopoly to publish printed part songs and to produce lined music manuscript paper.

Monopolies were justified on the grounds that they encouraged innovation, by protecting what today would be described as the intellectual property of the inventor. Of course, they were also a handy way of rewarding those who had performed a particular service for the queen.

Among the monopolies granted between 1574 and 1601, when the issue was debated in the House of Commons, Elizabeth I permitted the following: to print almanacs; to print David's Psalms; to print the history of Cornelius Tacitus; to make glasses; to collect customs duties [tonnage and poundage] on wines (a valuable monopoly granted to the queen's favourite, Sir Walter Raleigh); to make stone-pots; to provide steel beyond the seas; to print school books; to provide, bring, make and sell cards; and to make mathematical instruments.

Most Faithful Subject

During the reign of Queen Mary many Protestants refused to accept the possibility of the country being returned wholeheartedly to Catholicism and in February 1554, when Elizabeth was 20, she was arrested – first following a conspiracy against her half-sister, the queen, and then a full-scale rebellion in which Sir Thomas Wyatt led 3,000 Kentish men to the gates of London. The rebels declared that their intention was to prevent the queen marrying another Catholic monarch: Philip of Spain. Its real purpose, though, may well have been to overthrow Mary and put Elizabeth on the throne in her place.

On the morning of 17 March 1554, Elizabeth wrote to Mary at the palace of Westminster, where she had been confined for about a month. Mary had decided to send her half-sister to the Tower of London, where many traitors had ended their days; this letter was Elizabeth's plea to be allowed to see Mary to plead her innocence face-to-face before it was too late.

'If any ever did try this old saying – that a King's word was more than another man's oath – I most humbly beseech your majesty to verify it in me, and to remember your last promise and my last demand: that I be not condemned without answer and due proof. Which seems that now I am, for that, without cause proved, I am by your Council from you commanded to go unto the Tower, a place more wonted [appropriate] for a false traitor than a true subject. Which though I know I deserve it not, yet in this realm appears that it is proved. Which I pray God I may die the shamefullest death that ever any died before I may mean any such thing … And therefore I humbly beseech your majesty to let me answer before yourself and not suffer me to trust your councillors – yes, and that before I go to the Tower (if it be possible) if not, before I be further condemned …

I humbly crave one word of answer from yourself

Your highness' most faithful subject that has been from the beginning and will be to mine end,

Elizabeth'

(Despite this pleading, Mary did not respond to the letter and Elizabeth was sent to the Tower the following day, where she endured more than a month of anxious incarceration before being released without charge.)

Musical Appreciation

'Dr Tye [the composer and organist at the Chapel Royal] was a peevish and humoursome man, especially in his latter days, and sometimes playing on the organ in the chapel of Qu, Eliz. Which contained much music, but little delight to the ear, she would send the verger to tell him that he played out of tune, whereupon he sent word that her ears were out of tune.'

Antony à Wood, *Fasti Oxoniensis*

The Music Lovers

'The queen's will being to know the music, her Grace was at that time at the virginals: whereupon, being in attendance, Master Bull [organist at that time at the Chapel Royal] did come by stealth to hear without, and by mischance did sprawl into the queen's majesty's presence, to the queen's great disturbance. She demanding incontinent wherefore such presumption, Master Bull with great skill said that wheresoever majesty and music so well combined, no man might abase himself too deeply; whereupon the queen's majesty was mollified.'

Peter Phillips, *A Brief Chronicale*

National Rejoicing

The defeat of the Spanish Armada in 1588 was followed by national rejoicing, which reached a climax in November, when St Elizabeth's Day (19 November) and the days following were given over to celebrations and pageants.

The queen's popularity with her people had never been greater and wherever she went cheering crowds gathered. One occasion, recorded by an eyewitness in London, was typical of scenes repeated throughout that autumn.

'When the court gates were set open, no man did hinder us from coming in … [And after] we had stayed there an hour and a half and the yard was full, there being a great number of torches, the Queen came out in great state. Then we cried again, "God save your Majesty!" Then the Queen said again unto us: "God bless you all, my good people!" Then we cried again: "God save your Majesty!" Then the Queen said again unto us: "You may well have a greater prince, but you shall never have a more loving prince." And so, looking one upon another a while, the Queen departed. This wrought such an impression upon us, for shows and pageants are ever best seen by torch-light, that all the way along we did nothing but talk what an admirable Queen she was, and how we would adventure our lives to do her service.'

On Her Majesty's Service

As Queen Elizabeth's ambassador to Flanders, Valentine Dale found himself running short of money. However, he knew perfectly well that the queen was notoriously tight-fisted and that he was very likely to become seriously embarrassed for cash before funds reached him. Even so, he carried out his duties, writing to Elizabeth to outline affairs of state as he saw them, and mentioning in passing his financial situation. In the same packet he also sent an affectionate note to his wife: an intimate account of how he was getting on, which also expressed concern about his financial predicament.

As it turned out, the letter intended for his wife was addressed to the queen and vice versa, so Elizabeth was amazed and then amused to find her ambassador writing to her with endearments such as 'sweetheart' and 'dear love'. Although she quickly appreciated what had happened, Dale's financial problem appealed to her sense of diplomatic honour. Straight away she sent off additional supplies of money, little suspecting that the mix-up over the letters had been a deliberate ploy on the part of the artful diplomat.

A Prisoner's Lament

During the reign of Mary I, Elizabeth spent almost a year living under what amounted to house arrest in the royal hunting lodge at Woodstock. While she was there, she inscribed this woeful couplet, cut with a diamond on a window pane:

> *Much suspected by me,*
> *Nothing proved can be,*
> Quoth ELIZABETH prisoner

During the same period of imprisonment, Elizabeth wrote this poem on a wall at Woodstock:

> *O Fortune! how thy restless wavering State*
> *Hath fraught with Cares my troubled Wit!*
> *Witness this present Prison whither Fate*
> *Hath borne me, and the Joys I quit.*
> *Thou causedst the Guilty to be loosed*
> *From Bands, wherewith are Innocents inclosed;*
> *Causing the Guiltless to be strait reserved,*
> *And freeing those that Death had well deserved:*
> *But by her Envy can be nothing wrought,*
> *So God send to my Foes all they have thought.*
> ELIZABETH PRISONER

Privy Council

For Tudor monarchs the privy council acted like a present-day cabinet, or a board of directors, who advised the monarch and oversaw the administration of state business. Where Queen Mary had a privy council numbering around 50, Elizabeth cut this significantly to 19. Out went most of the clergy who had served Mary, signalling that religion would no longer have a contolling hand in affairs of state.

The team Elizabeth gathered around her was a coalition of all the principal factions in her realm: a balance of nobility and the rising merchant class, a microcosm of the country as a whole.

The new queen stamped her authority on her new council at its first official meeting on 20 November 1558, at which she told them:

'I give you this charge, that you shall be of my Privy Council, and content yourself to take pains for me and my realm. This judgement I have of you, that you will not be corrupted with any manner of gift, and that you will be favourable to the state, and that, without respect of my private will, you will give me that counsel that you think best. And if you shall know anything necessary to be declared to me of secrecy, you shall show it to myself only, and assure yourself I will not fail to keep taciturnity therein.'

Prophetic Judgement

'God has given you great qualities. Cultivate them always, and labour to improve them, for I believe you are destined by Heaven to be Queen of England.'

Words reputedly spoken by Catherine Parr to her stepdaughter, Princess Elizabeth, in May 1547

The Queen and the Bard

'It is well known that Queen Elizabeth was a great admirer of the immortal Shakespeare, and used frequently (as was the custom with persons of great rank in those days) to appear upon the stage before the audience, or to sit delighted behind the scenes, when the plays of our bard were performed. One evening, when Shakespeare himself was personating the part of a King, the audience knew of her Majesty being in the house. She crossed the stage when he was performing, and, on receiving the accustomed greeting from the audience, moved politely to the poet, but he did not notice it! When behind the scenes, she caught his eye, and moved again, but still he would not throw off his character, to notice her: this made her Majesty think of some means by which she might know, whether he would depart or not, from the dignity of his character, while on the stage. Accordingly, as he was about to make his exit, she stepped before him, dropped her glove, and re-crossed the stage, which, Shakespeare noticing it, took up, with these words, immediately after finishing his speech, and so aptly were they delivered, that they seemed to belong in it:

> And though now bent on this high embassy,
> Yet stoop we to take up our *Cousin's* glove!

He then walked off the stage, and presented the glove to the Queen, who was greatly pleased with his behaviour, and complimented him upon the propriety of it.'

Anonymous

The Queen's Frog

This was the amorous nickname that Elizabeth gave to Francis, duke of Alençon and Anjou and brother of King Henry III of France. Although he was 20 years her junior, the queen appeared genuinely captivated by the

63

charming and intelligent (if physically rather unprepossessing) French prince when he was her suitor from 1579 until 1582. When a marriage to a Catholic was ruled to be politically impossible the couple parted, but the queen's disappointment was keenly expressed in this poem, written after her French suitor had left England for the last time:

> *ON MONSIEUR'S DEPARTURE*
>
> *I grieve and dare not show my discontent,*
> *I love and yet am forced to seem to hate,*
> *I do, yet dare not say I ever meant,*
> *I seem stark mute but inwardly do prate.*
> *I am and not, I freeze and yet am burned,*
> *Since from myself another self I turned.*
> *My care is like my shadow in the sun,*
> *Follows me flying, flies when I pursue it,*
> *Stands and lies by me, doth what I have done.*
> *His too familiar care doth make me rue it.*
> *No means I find to rid him from my breast,*
> *Till by the end of things it be supprest.*
> *Some gentler passion slide into my mind,*
> *For I am soft and made of melting snow;*
> *Or be more cruel, love, and so be kind.*
> *Let me or float or sink, be high or low.*
> *Or let me live with some more sweet content,*
> *Or die and so forget what love ere meant.*

The Queen's Image

From the early years of her reign, Elizabeth I was concerned about the way she was portrayed in pictures. In order to achieve a satisfactory continuity of appearance Sir Robert Cecil, her secretary of state, instituted an element of 'quality control'. 'Many painters have done portraits of the Queen,' he wrote, 'but none has sufficiently shown her looks or charms. Therefore Her Majesty commands all manner of persons to stop doing portraits of her until a clever painter has finished one which all other painters can copy. Her Majesty, in the meantime, forbids the showing of any portraits which are ugly until they are improved.'

The Queen Is Dead – Long Live the Queen

'This is the Lord's doing and it is marvellous in our eyes.'
Biblical verse reputedly spoken in Latin by Elizabeth I when she received news of her accession to the throne following the death of Queen Mary

Ravages of Smallpox

In the autumn of 1562 Elizabeth I contracted smallpox. According to a contemporary author on medical matters, this was a 'common and familiar' disease, 'called of ye small pocks … The signs are itch and fretting of the skin as if it had been rubbed with nettles, pain in the head and back etc: sometimes as it were a dry scab or lepry spreading over all the members, other whiles in pushes, pimples and whayls running with much corruption and matter, and with great pains of the face and throat, dryness of the tongue, hoarseness of the voice …'

The queen was fortunate to recover with few blemishes to her pale skin, but Lady Mary Sidney, who had been nursing her, suffered the full ravages of the disease. 'I left her a full fair lady, in mine eyes at least the fairest,' said her husband, 'and when I returned I found her as foul a lady as the smallpox could make her, which she did take by continued attendance upon her Majesty's most precious person.'

Read My Lips

On the morning of 8 February 1586, Mary, Queen of Scots, went to her execution in Fotheringay Castle, in Northamptonshire. Among those who witnessed the scene was Robert Wynkfielde, who vividly recorded the event.

'Her prayers being ended, the executioners, kneeling, desired her Grace to forgive them her death: who answered, "I forgive you with all my heart, for now, I hope, you shall make an end of all my troubles." Then they, with her two women, helping her up, began to disrobe her of her apparel …

Then she, lying very still upon the block, one of the executioners holding slightly with one of his hands, she endured two strokes of the other executioner with an axe, she making very small noise or none at all, and not stirring any part of her from the place where she lay: and so the executioner cut off her head, saving one little gristle, which being cut asunder, he lift up her head to the view of all the assembly and bade *God save the Queen*. Then, her dress of lawn falling from off her head, it appeared as grey as one of threescore and ten years old, polled very short, her face in a moment being so much altered from the form she had when she was alive, as few could remember her by her dead face. Her lips stirred up and down a quarter of an hour after her head was cut off.'

Regal Disdain

Not long after Elizabeth I came to the throne, a knight who had treated her with contempt during the previous reign of her half-sister Mary – when Elizabeth was living in disgrace and obscurity – threw himself at her feet to beseech her pardon.

The queen gestured to him to rise and then dismissed him with the comment, 'Do you not know that we are descended of the lion, whose nature is not to prey upon the mouse or any other such small vermin.'

A Rival Queen on Trial

'To Mary, Queen of Scots, October 1586

You have in various ways and manners attempted to take my life and to bring my kingdom to destruction by bloodshed. I have never proceeded so harshly against you, but have, on the contrary, protected and maintained you like myself. These treasons will be proved to you and all made manifest. Yet it is my will, that you answer the nobles and peers of the kingdom as if I were myself present. I therefore require, charge, and command that you make answer for I have been well informed of your arrogance.

Act plainly without reserve, and you will sooner be able to obtain favour of me. Elizabeth'

Translation of a letter, written in French, from Elizabeth I to Mary, Queen of Scots, sent at the opening of her trial for plotting against Elizabeth in October 1586

In contrast to this letter from the queen of England, Mary told her jailer, Sir Amyas Paulet, 'As a sinner I am truly conscious of having often offended my Creator and I beg him to forgive me, but as a Queen and Sovereign, I am aware of no fault or offence for which I have to render account to anyone here below.'

Mary was eloquent in defending herself against the charges laid before her, but she retained her regal dignity to the end:

'I am myself a Queen, the daughter of a King, a stranger, and the true Kinswoman of the Queen of England. I came to England on my cousin's promise of assistance against my enemies and rebel subjects and was at once imprisoned ... As an absolute Queen, I cannot submit to orders, nor can I submit to the laws of the land without injury to myself, the King my son and all other sovereign princes ... For myself I do not recognise the laws of England nor do I know or understand them as I have often asserted. I am alone without counsel, or anyone to speak on my behalf. My papers and notes have been taken from me, so that I am destitute of all aid, taken at a disadvantage ...

There is not one, I think, among you, let him be the cleverest man you will, but would be incapable of resisting or defending himself were he in my place …

I have desired nothing but my own deliverance … my subjects became sad and haughty and abused my clemency; indeed they now complain that they were never so well off as under my government … My lords and gentlemen, I place my cause in the hands of God … May God keep me from having to do with you all again.'

Royal Appetites

In 1577 Queen Elizabeth spent three days at Lord North's house, in the course of which the assembled company ate prodigiously. One commentator noted that: '67 sheep and 34 pigs were consumed; 4 stags and 16 bucks were used to make 176 pasties; 1,200 chickens, 363 capons, 33 geese, 6 turkeys, 237 dozen pigeons and quantities of partridges, pheasants, snip and all kinds of other birds, including gulls; a cartload and two horseloads of oysters, fish in endless variety, 2,500 eggs and 430 pounds of butter.'

Royal Favour

Richard Hakluyt, the Elizabethan geographer and historian, recorded an account of Sir Francis Drake given by the Spanish noble, Don Francisco da Zarate. Drake, Zarate said, 'is served on silver dishes with gold borders and gilded garlands, in which are his arms. He said that many of these had been given him by the Queen.'

Royal Progress

In an age when communication was slow, a royal journey, or progress, was a satisfactory way of allowing the people of England to see their queen. It also provided the shrewd Elizabeth with a means of keeping her wealthiest nobles in check, by obliging them to spend significant sums of money entertaining her and her retinue when they came to stay.

Elizabeth I's progresses usually lasted eight to 12 weeks and in one summer (1578) the queen and court stayed at 25 different places and dined in 10 others. In addition to the queen and her immediate staff, the entire court was expected to take to the road, amounting to a caravan of 200 to 300 carts containing everything from the queen's sizeable wardrobe to any legal documents that might be needed.

Expeditions of this kind required months of planning and preparations began early in the year, when court officials went on a tour of inspection to visit houses at which the queen intended to stay, and to ensure that there were no outbreaks of the plague in their vicinity. The priority was to find suitable accommodation for the queen herself; only after that had been identified were suitable lodgings found for the rest of the court. When all this had been arranged, the planned itinerary, or 'geste', was published, listing all the places where the queen would be residing, though not any specific dates when she would be in residence. Copies of the geste were then sent to local officials along the route, whose duty it was to confirm that the areas under their jurisdiction were still free of plague. After this the royal purveyors arrived, demanding stocks of food, fuel and fodder, which were then officially purchased by a yeoman purveyor.

On the road, it was the responsibility of the queen's gentlemen ushers to organise the public rooms she would be using, checking that only those authorised to do so were allowed to enter them. They, with the officers of the wardrobe, had the unenviable task of making the queen feel at home all along the route.

When she arrived at a new destination, the queen expected her apartments to be ready. Likewise, no packing was permitted until after she had departed. As a result the ushers and wardrobe staff worked in relays, with one team packing up after a royal visit while another had hurried ahead to be ready to receive Her Majesty when she arrived.

Royal Temper

'When she smiled it was pure sunshine, that everyone did choose to bask in, if they could; but anon came a storm from a sudden gathering of clouds, and the thunder fell in a wondrous manner on all alike.'

Sir John Harington, Queen Elizabeth's godson

The Scottish Heir

'Dear Son, I send three bearers to see you and bring me word how ye do, and to remember you that ye have in me a loving mother that wishes you to learn in time to love know and fear God.'

To her son, from Mary, Queen of Scots – the note never reached him

'The Queen of Scots is lighter of a fair son, and I am but a barren stock.'

Elizabeth I speaking at the time of the birth of the future James I

'I have borne him and God Knoweth with what danger to him and to me both, and of you he is descended, so I mean not to forget my duty to you.'
To Lady Lennox, James's grandmother, from Mary, Queen of Scots

Sea Causes

Elizabeth I's father, King Henry VIII, had done a great deal to develop the English navy. During his reign the number of ships the sovereign could call on in times of war rose from six or seven to more than 50. Henry also established a Council for Marine Causes, to manage both the fleet and dockyards where they were maintained and equipped. Although the number of ships had dropped to around 40 by the time she came to the throne, Elizabeth still inherited a fighting force on which future national sea power could be built.

Shortly after her accession, the queen commissioned a naval survey, *The Book of Sea Causes*, to establish in her own mind the state of the navy, but also to understand the costs of mobilisation. An indication of the costs involved are given in this extract:

Charges for putting the army in order:
The charges of which army, as well for the prest [advance payments] and conduct of the men, rigging, wages, victuals and provisions of all kind till

the joining of the said army at a place certain, will amount in estimation to:

£10,152 13s 4d

The charge of the whole army being furnished shall be:
Item the monthly charges of the foresaid army being joined and full furnished in fashion of war will be £11,363, which for five months will amount to 8s 6d wages and 12s victuals a man per mensem [every month] with 12d a ton for tonnage of the merchant ships, the sum of: £56,856

The charge of dissolving the army:
Item at the dissolving of the army the transporting of the Queen's Majesty's ships and the merchants' to their several harbours, with the conduct of the rest of the men which have then to be discharged out of them, with other extraordinary charges, will amount in estimation to:

£4,000

£71,377 0s 12d [*sic*]

(Arithmetic was often inaccurate in 16th-century documents such as this because of the continued use of Roman numerals.)

Self Control

'Anger makes dull men witty, but it keeps them poor.'

Elizabeth to Sir Edward Dyer

'A strength to harm is perilous in the hand of an ambitious head.'

Elizabeth in a letter to Henry Sidney, 1565

'What availeth wit when it fails the owner at greatest need?'

Elizabeth criticising Robert Dudley for using the discretion she had given him when representing her in the Netherlands

'I regret the unhappiness of princes who are slaves to forms and fettered by caution.'

Elizabeth to King Henry IV of France, 1601

Servants of the Crown

'I shall desire you all, my lords, (chiefly you of the nobility, everyone in his degree and power) to be assistant to me that I, with my ruling, and you with your service, may make a good account to Almighty God and leave some comfort to our posterity on earth.'

Elizabeth to her nobles, at the beginning of her reign

'Let this my discipline stand you in good stead of sorer strokes, never to tempt too far a Prince's patience.'

Elizabeth to Parliament

'Unbridled persons whose mouths were never snaffled by the rider, did rashly ride.'

Elizabeth to Parliament, reasserting her authority in 1566

Speak Now or Forever Hold Your Peace

When, in 1578, it looked likely that Elizabeth I might marry the Catholic duke of Alençon and Anjou, many of her Protestant subjects were dismayed. In August of the following year, John Stubbs gave voice to their fears in a political pamphlet which he entitled *The Discoverie of a Gaping Gulf*. This caused the queen great offence, as the antiquarian and historian William Camden recorded.

'Her Majesty … burned with choler that there was a book published in print inveighing against the marriage, as fearing the alteration of religion … Neither would Queen Elizabeth be persuaded that the author of the book had any other purpose but to bring her into hatred with her subjects, and to open a gap to some prodigious innovation.

… within a few days after, John Stubbs of Lincoln's Inn, a zealous professor of religion, the author of this relative pamphlet (whose sister Thomas Cartwright the arch-Puritan had married), William Page the dispenser of copies, and Singleton the printer were apprehended: against whom sentence was given that their right hands should be cut off by a law in the time of Philip and Mary against the authors of *seditious writings*, and those that disperse them …

Not long after, upon a stage set up in the market place at Westminster,

Stubbs and Page had their right hands cut off by the blow of a butcher's knife with a mallet struck through their wrists. The printer had his pardon. I can remember that, standing by John Stubbs, so soon as his right hand was cut off he put off his hat with the left, and cried aloud, 'God save the Queen!' The people round him stood mute, whether stricken with fear at the first sight of this strange punishment, or out of a secret inward repining they had at this marriage, which they suspected would be dangerous to religion.'

Standing to the Last

There used to be a belief that a king should die standing. Perhaps for this reason it is said that Elizabeth I refused to lie on her deathbed at Richmond Palace. She eventually collapsed on to cushions and died just before 3.00 am on 24 March 1603.

According to the royal chaplain, Dr Henry Parry, it was a 'good death', as 'hir Majestie departed this lyfe, mildly like a lambe, easily like a ripe apple from the tree …'

The Suitor's Lot

Edmund Spenser satirised life at Court in *Mother Hubberd's Tale*, in which he commented on the miseries endured by royal suitors:

> *To lose good days that better might be spent;*
> *To waste long nights in pensive discontent;*
> *To spend today, to be put back tomorrow;*
> *To feed on hope, to pine with fear and sorrow;*
> *To have thy Prince's grace, yet want her Peers;*
> *To have thy asking, yet wait many years …*

Survival Instincts

In spite of rumours of plots centred on Mary, Queen of Scots during her 18 years' imprisonment in England, Elizabeth showed great reluctance in agreeing to repeated suggestions that Mary should be executed. Even though she did eventually sign her death warrant, she did so very unwillingly.

'What will my enemies not say, that for the safety of her life a maiden queen could be content to spill the blood even of her own kinswoman?'

Elizabeth to a parliamentary delegation in 1586, eager for her to proceed with the execution of Mary, Queen of Scots

～

'Your judgement I condemn not, neither do I mistake your reasons, but pray you to accept my thankfulness, excuse my doubtfulness, and take in good part my answer, answerless.'

Elizabeth to a parliamentary delegation again in regard to the execution of Mary, Queen of Scots

～

'You lawyers are so nice and precise in shifting and scanning every word and letter that many times you stand more upon form than matter, upon syllables than the sense of the law.'

Elizabeth to lawyers urging her to execute the Queen of Scots

Symbolic Significance

Portraits of Elizabeth I frequently display symbols representing emblematic features of her character or public status. Among the most common of these are:

Armillary spheres – devices used to study the movement of the planets, which represented wisdom and power and were also emblematic of harmony between Elizabeth and her subjects.

Crowns, orbs and sceptres – royal regalia signifying monarchy.

Dogs – representative of faithfulness, the greyhound in particular was associated with the Tudor royal line.

Ermine – legend holds that the ermine would rather die than soil its pure white coat; as a consequence it came to symbolise purity. The wearing of ermine was restricted to royalty and nobility, so in portraits of Elizabeth it also acts as a status symbol.

Gloves – fine gloves were often presented to the queen as prestigious presents and as such they represent elegance in portraits of her.

Moons – in ancient mythology the moon goddess, Diana, was a virgin and therefore a symbol of purity. Diana was also known as Cynthia and Sir Walter Raleigh's poem *The Ocean's Love to Cynthia*, in which he compared Elizabeth I to the moon, helped to popularise the connection between the Virgin Queen and the virgin deity of ancient mythology.

Olive branches – traditional symbols of peace.

Pearls – from their resemblance to the moon, pearls acquired the same figurative attributes and came to represent virginity and purity.

Pelicans – mother pelicans were believed to save their dying young in times of food shortage by plucking at their own breasts and sustaining their offspring with their blood, though dying in the process. This self-sacrifice became associated in the Middle Ages with the sacrifice made by Jesus on the cross. So the pelican became a favourite symbol for Elizabeth I, representing her motherly care for her subjects.

Phoenixes – the phoenix is a mythological bird that never dies, though after 500 years it is consumed by fire to be born again in the flames. As a symbol of endurance and eternal life, it became emblematic of the

Resurrection and, as only one phoenix lives at a time, it became a symbol of Elizabeth I's longevity and unique status.

Sieves – a legend from ancient Rome tells of Tuccia, a vestal virgin, who reputedly proved her virginity by carrying water in a sieve without spilling a drop. As a result the sieve became an icon of virginity and virtue and, in the case of Elizabeth I, associated her reign with the glorious days of ancient Rome.

Tudor roses – the Tudor dynasty established by Elizabeth's grandfather, Henry VII, was symbolised by a red and white rose. This had been created by combining the emblems of the two rival factions in the Wars of the Roses: the red rose of Lancaster and the white rose of York. In 1486 the two houses were united by the marriage of the Lancastrian Henry VII and Elizabeth of York, and the Tudor rose came into being as a symbol of unity. The rose was also a symbol of the Virgin Mary, so the Tudor rose neatly linked the Virgin Queen with her.

terror and triumph in the Tower

As queen, Elizabeth I must have looked on the Tower of London with very mixed emotions; for the Tower had witnessed the most terrifying and triumphant episodes of her life.

On 18 March 1554 she passed through Traitors' Gate and was taken to the Bell Tower as a prisoner of her half-sister, Queen Mary. A few weeks earlier she had been incriminated in a plot against Mary; the allegation was untrue, but in the highly charged atmosphere in which Mary came to the throne, it was thought that Princess Elizabeth might become the focus of a wider rebellion. While she was captive in the Tower, efforts were made to make her convert to the Roman Catholic faith, but she refused. Like other captives before her, the confinement of her prison affected her health, though she was fortunate in being allowed to walk on the ramparts between the Bell and Beauchamp Towers, which is still known as Princess Elizabeth's Walk. Two months later, when no evidence against her had been produced, she was released.

Three years later, after Mary had died, Elizabeth rode into London as the new queen and went to the Tower. When she arrived, she patted the earth and said, 'Some have fallen from being princes of this land to be prisoners in this place. I am raised from being a prisoner in this place to be a prince of the land.'

On that occasion, she stayed in the Tower for a week while she appointed her ministers, and returned in January 1559 to spend three days preparing for her coronation.

Then Came Her Grace

Before her coronation, Elizabeth I travelled to the Tower of London to spend a vigil. The procession that bore her through the city was one of the most splendid the capital had ever witnessed. A contemporary account records that it was 'headed by gentlemen and knights and lords and after came all the trumpets blowing and then came all the heralds in array and my Lord of Pembroke bore the Queen's sword. Then came her Grace on horseback in purple velvet with a sash around her neck and sergeants-at-arms about her Grace. And next after rode Robert Dudley, her master of horse and so the guard with halberds. There was such shooting of guns as never was heard before.'

Tilts and Tournaments

National festivals such as St George's Day, and those associated with Queen Elizabeth herself – her birthday and the anniversary of her accession – became almost as popular during her reign as the great feast days of the Christian Church.

Magnificent tournaments were staged at the royal palaces, drawing 'many thousand spectators'. A German visitor to an Accession Day tournament recorded these details of the combatants taking part and the bands of servants accompanying them:

'Others had horses equipped like elephants. Some carriages were drawn by men, others appeared to move by themselves … When a gentleman and his horses approached the barrier, on horseback or in a carriage, he stopped at the foot of the staircase leading to the Queen's room, while one of his servants in pompous attire mounted the steps and addressed the Queen in well-composed verse or with a ludicrous speech, making her and her ladies laugh. When the speech was ended he offered the Queen a costly present in the name of his lord. [Then the contestants] rose against each other, breaking lances across the beam.'

True Love

'I do not want a husband who honours me as a queen, if he does not love me as a woman.'

Elizabeth to the French ambassador

'Although my royal rank causes me to doubt whether my kingdom is not more sought after than myself, yet I understand that you have found other graces in me'.

Elizabeth to Francis, duke of Alençon and Anjou, around 1572

The Virgin Queen

'I am more afraid of making a fault in my Latin than of the Kings of Spain, France, Scotland, and the whole house of Guise, and of all their confederates.'

Elizabeth on herself

'I would rather be a beggar and single than a queen and married.'

Elizabeth on herself

Wardrobe Mistress

Despite the severe manner of her dress as a young woman, when she regularly appeared dressed simply in black or white, Queen Elizabeth I was as fond of fine clothes and jewels as her father had been. In 1599 alone £700 was spent 'on fine linen for her Majesty's person'. Towards the end of her life an inventory of the royal wardrobe recorded a dazzling array of clothes, which included: 102 'French gownes', 100 'loose gownes', 67 'rounde gownes', 99 robes, 127 cloaks, 85 doublets, 125 petticoats, 56 'saufgardes [outer skirts] and juppes', 126 kirtles, 18 'lappe mantles' and 136 'foreparts' [stomachers].

Warning From History

'Twenty years later, when England and the courts of Europe were agog with the idea that Queen Elizabeth might marry the Earl of Leicester, Lord Leicester told the French Ambassador that he had known Elizabeth since she was a child of eight, and from that very time she had always said, "I will never marry." Little notice was paid to the words. It did not occur to anyone it seems, to look back and recall that when Elizabeth was eight years and five months old, Catherine Howard was beheaded.'

Elizabeth Jenkins, *Elizabeth the Great*

What's in a Name?

In 1547 Matthew Parker, who was consecrated archbishop of Canterbury 12 years later, married Margaret Harlestone of Mattishall, Norfolk, to whom he had been betrothed for seven years but had been unable to marry while the law forbade the marriage of clergymen. Even though this was altered by the House of Convocation, Queen Elizabeth retained her strong disapproval. On one occasion she found it necessary to thank the archbishop's wife, and did so by writing, 'Madam I may not call you; mistress I am ashamed to call you; and so I know not what to call you; but, howsoever, I thank you.'

(Not everyone shared the queen's view of marriage for the clergy. Margaret Harlestone proved to be such an admirable wife that another bishop asked whether she had a sister.)

Your Humble Servant

Since the 12th century it had been a custom on Maundy Thursday for the English sovereign to kiss the feet of a group of poor people, in memory of Jesus Christ who did this for his disciples at the Last Supper. The practice was said to have been instigated by Henry I's 'good Queen Maud'. Elizabeth I was rather more particular, however, and she had the feet of the poor washed before handling them to perform the token ceremony herself. She also changed the presenting of a royal gown into a gift of money.

The End

Elizabeth I was given a funeral in keeping with the ceremony and opulence of her reign. Four horses draped in black drew the carriage on which her coffin, covered in purple velvet, was laid. As with all such royal funerals, a robed effigy of the late monarch, scepter in hand, was placed on top of the coffin. With the queen's body hidden from view, the effigy remained as a tangible representation of her status and authority. And the life-like effigy moved to tears many of the people lining the streets to see her pass.

The chronicler, John Stow, attended the funeral and wrote, 'Westminster was surcharged with multitudes of all sorts of people in their streets, houses, windows, leads and gutters, that came to see the obsequy, and when they beheld her statue lying upon the coffin, there was such a general sighing, groaning and weeping as the like hath not been seen or known in the memory of man, neither doth any history mention any people, time or state to make like lamentation for the death of their sovereign.'

Elizabeth I had not been long dead when her virtues as ruler of the English people began to be contrasted favourably with what many saw as the shortcomings of her successor, James I. 'When we had experience of [King James's] government,' wrote the bishop of Gloucester, Godfrey Goodman, 'the Queen did seem to revive. Then was her memory much magnified: such ringing of bells, such public joy and sermons in commemoration of her, the picture of her tomb painted in many churches, and in effect more solemnity and joy in memory of her coronation than ever was for the coming-in of King James.'